Hobo and the Frisbee

Daniel England

 FriesenPress

Suite 300 - 990 Fort St
Victoria, BC, V8V 3K2
Canada

www.friesenpress.com

ISBN
978-1-4602-8840-5 (Paperback)
978-1-4602-8841-2 (eBook)

1. JUVENILE NONFICTION, ANIMALS, DOGS

Distributed to the trade by The Ingram Book Company

This is a story
about a little dog
named Hobo.

This is Hobo.

Little Hobo knew how to fetch. He liked the ball. He liked to fetch.

He was a very smart dog.
Hobo's people could tell that he
was a very special dog.

One day, Hobo's people wanted to teach him to catch a Frisbee—but how?!

"How do we teach this dog?"
the people said.

"This dog cannot speak to us.

This dog does not understand
what we say to him."

6

When a person says:
"Let's go to the dog park today."

A dog hears:
"Blah, blah, **DOG PARK**, blah, blah."

what to do?

"We've got it!" the people said.

What do you do when you have to do something overwhelming, something that's really hard?

Break it into steps!
Solve it piece by piece, bit by bit.

"We will teach him the steps!" the people said.
"Yes, we will teach him to catch a Frisbee bit by bit."

Hobo already knew how to fetch, so that was good.

But he would have to learn to catch something in the air.

And he would have to learn to run and watch it while it was coming to him.

12

So, they started
to teach him...

First, one person held little Hobo still.

So still that he could not run.

Then a friend tossed the ball to Hobo.

He tossed the ball from close by.
Very close by.

Look at your fingers.

As long as your fingers are, that's how far away
they were when they tossed the ball to Hobo.

It was very hard for Hobo.
Hobo wanted to run.
Hobo wanted to fetch.

Hobo did NOT want the ball to be tossed
while he was held and could not run.

And he told them so!

Bark!

Bark!

Bark!

Bark!

Bark!

Bark!

"Bark!" Hobo said. Which of course means: "I want the ball!"
"Bark, Bark!" Hobo said. Which of course means: "I want to run!"
"Bark, Bark, Bark!"
Hobo said. Which of course means: "I want to fetch!"

Little Hobo really wanted the ball.

Hobo wanted the ball so much that he tried to grab it with his mouth when they tossed it.

He tried and tried.

And tried and tried...

Then,
all of a sudden...

He caught it!

Then...
he caught it again!

The people backed up and tried from **FartHer** away.

Look at your arms.

As long as your arms are,

that's how far away they were when they tossed the ball to Hobo.

Hobo tried and tried...

Then, all of the sudden,
he caught it!

Then he caught it **again!**

Now it was time for the Frisbee.

The people backed up again.
This time they were really far away.

Look at your room.

As long as your room is, that's how far away
they were when they tossed the ball to Hobo.
Only this time, it was not a ball...

It was the Frisbee!

The Frisbee was bright red. It was soft.

Hobo wanted that Frisbee.

"Sit, Hobo," they said.
"Stay, Hobo," they said.

Hobo did not want to sit or stay. Hobo wanted that Frisbee!

But Hobo was a good dog
and a smart dog.

So Hobo sat,
and Hobo stayed.

Hobo could see the Frisbee from across the yard.

Hobo wanted the Frisbee so bad that his lip began to quiver.

And then the people threw the Frisbee.

The Frisbee flew across the yard. It came closer
and closer to Hobo. He wanted the Frisbee.
Hobo wanted that Frisbee more than anything.

And then...

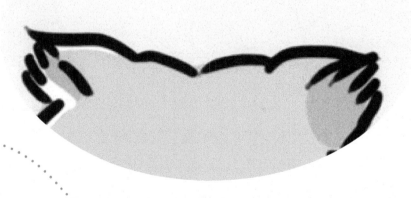

And then...

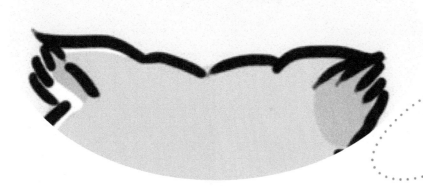

He caught it!

Hobo caught the Frisbee!

Hooray!

Hobo was so happy and proud that he ran all around the yard with the Frisbee in mouth.

Now Hobo would teach his people a new game. And that game was called...

Keep away!

Bark, Bark.

The End.

For the groWN-UpS:

Hobo is a real dog. He weighs nine pounds and is five years old at the time of publishing.

Hobo was adopted from the Riverside Humane Society, in Riverside, California.

If you would like to donate to the Riverside Humane Society, please visit:
http://www.petsadoption.com/index.php/giving/donations/general

All of Hobo's stories are true, more or less. ;)

You can watch videos of Hobo catching his Frisbee by searching YouTube.com for "9poundsofawesomeness."

CPSIA information can be obtained
at www.ICGtesting.com
Printed in the USA
BVOW05s1322011117
499243BV00027B/489/P